P9-AOD-714

# One Foot Forward

## Stories and Faces of Widows and Widowers

# One Foot Forward

## Stories and Faces of Widows and Widowers

Judith Fox

Foreword by Joanne Lynn, MD
Essay by Michele Reiss, PhD

# Introduction

My husband, Jerry Fox, was two weeks shy of his 54th birthday when he died from an inoperable adenocarcinoma of the lung. The oncologist had predicted that he might have six months before the aggressive cancer would take his life. But Jerry died on a lovely spring day—exactly one month after he was diagnosed. It was 12:30 in the afternoon and Jerry—who said he wasn't hungry—headed upstairs to our den to read. While I was eating a sandwich in our kitchen, my husband took his last breath; he was sitting in his favorite chair with a book by his side when I found his body. After the initial shock, I spent much of the following year in tears.

I was a relative innocent when it came to death and loss. After Jerry died, though, the scrim that had been in place between me and those around me suddenly dropped, revealing a universe of private hurt that had previously been concealed: one friend told me about the death of her child (seven years earlier) from a drug overdose; another told me about several painful miscarriages that she had never discussed; conversations with strangers immediately and easily extended into personal and painful corners. My life and my world had been altered—and deepened.

In time, I fell in love again, and three years after I was widowed I married Edmund Ackell. Three years later, the man I loved and shared my life with was diagnosed with Alzheimer's Disease.

I began photographing Ed in 2001 as part of a personal photography project. I had been a photographer and writer for several decades. Shortly after beginning that body of work, I found myself thinking often about Alzheimer's, mortality, love, commitment, and resilience—and I began creating the book that became *I Still Do: Loving and Living with Alzheimer's.*

In recent years, aware of the likelihood that I would be widowed again, and surrounded by friends who were being widowed for the first time, I began reflecting on the significant losses and changes that accompany the death of a spouse or partner. I had lived the experience, but I wanted to know more. I wanted to understand how others navigated widowhood and moved forward with hope. And I wanted to learn from—and tell the stories of—a diverse group of widows and widowers whose varied journeys would help me frame my own. So, I talked with people whose spouses died gradually and I talked with people whose spouses died suddenly; I conversed with the young, middle-aged, and elderly; I spoke with people who had been in complex marriages and people who had lived in marriages that were uncomplicated. *One Foot Forward* was born of personal knowledge and candid conversations with generous people who believe—as I do—in the power and solace of shared stories.

Judith Fox

# Foreword: Our Need for Stories

Joanne Lynn, MD

If grief for the death of someone dear were a country, no one would want to live there or even visit. But grief is a country that comes up on your itinerary unwanted, unavoidable. And when you arrive, you have little sense of when or how you will leave, or how the experience will change you. Some deaths in *One Foot Forward* were sudden, some quite complicated, and some seemed just a breath away for years. The poet John Stone, a physician himself, observed, "Death / I have seen / come on / slowly as rust / sand / or suddenly / as when / someone leaving / a room / finds the doorknob / come loose in his hand."

The death of a spouse—a person heavily interwoven into the very fabric of your life—is especially troubling. The anchors of everyday life go missing, and the widow or widower must keep living through minutes stripped of their meaning. Grief marks the other side of the coin of caring relationships. We cannot live a life enriched by the love and intimacy of a spouse without feeling the wrenching disorientation of that spouse's death. However, the response of a bereaved spouse to death shows remarkable variety. The character of the marriage and the particulars of the spouse's death undoubtedly affect the grieving, but not predictably. Each of us must find our way "home" in our own way.

One of the modern-day challenges facing survivors is the silence surrounding death. Our political leaders and movie stars rarely share their personal stories of dying, death, and grief. Our newspapers and television shows do not explain or instruct how survivors manage to get through this day, and then the next. Often, we are almost embarrassed to find that a person in our midst is bereaved; we are at a loss for words, even for appropriate platitudes. We need stories that can show us available paths and can teach us the language of healing.

This book collects a set of searing stories about the death of a spouse, illuminated by evocative photographs of the storytellers. It is not easy to read. The emotions are palpable, and the confusion, despair, and pain are sometimes overwhelming. But the stories here illuminate the miracle of enduring—stories of survival, gradually finding ways to reconnect with the world, and the arrival at an emotional standing where the widow or widower once again feels life is fulfilling.

The stories here can help make some of the experience of grieving a little more familiar, granting a measure of peace to widows and widowers and enabling others to relate to them more readily. Remarkably, most people do keep putting "one foot forward," and most even construct new and often more meaningful lives. In that sense, these are stories of triumph—of the human spirit finding a way to blossom, even in very difficult circumstances.

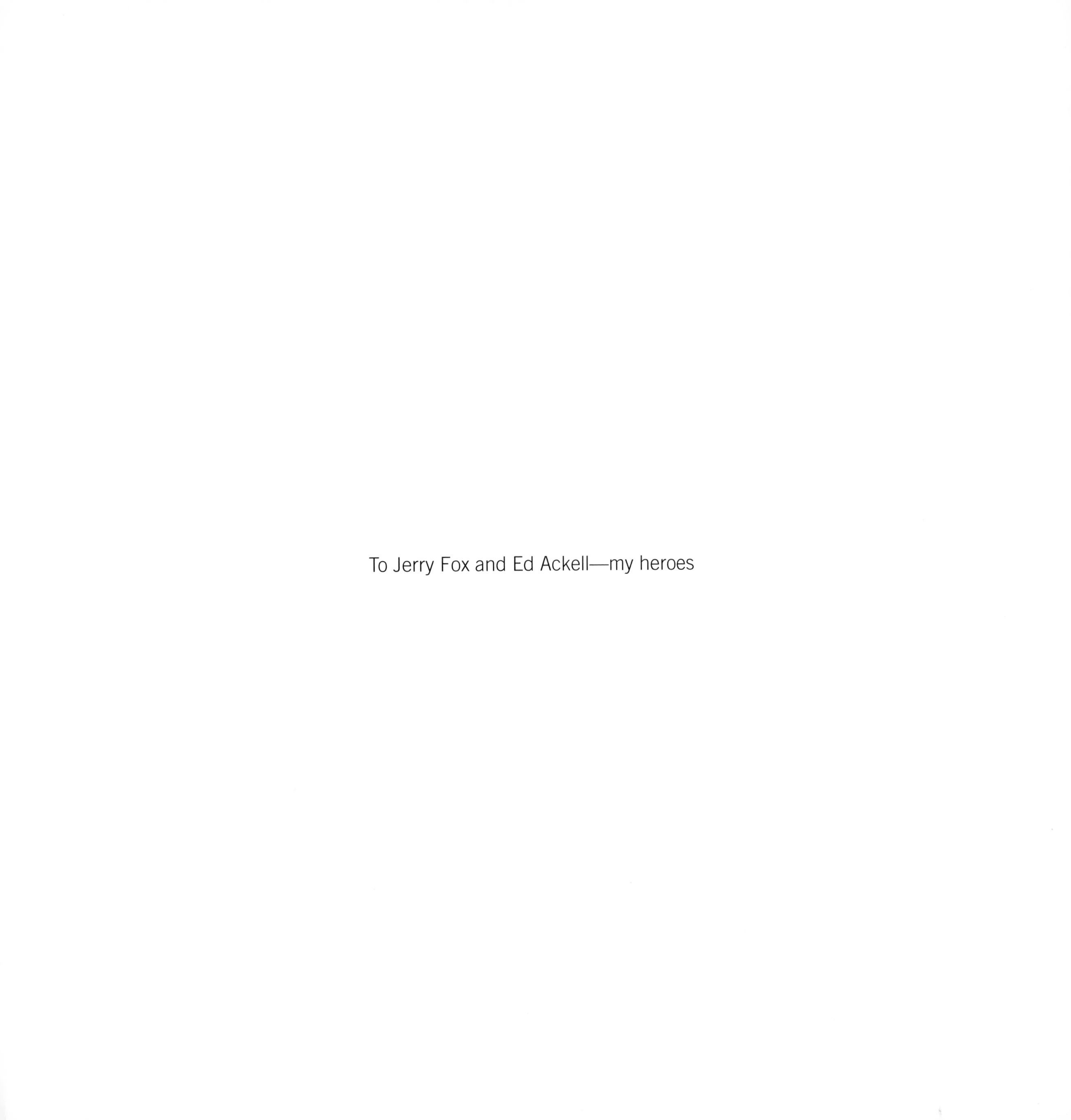

To Jerry Fox and Ed Ackell—my heroes

"The universe is made of stories, not of atoms."
Muriel Rukeyser,
*The Speed of Darkness*

# Susan
## Krahn

"I'm not ready to remarry.
But maybe someday."

# Susan
## Krahn

A wooden box was displayed—front and center—at Paul Krahn's funeral. The box, which was the size of a milk crate, was surrounded by flower arrangements, an 8x10 photograph of Paul, and some smaller pictures of him with his wife and three children. On one side, Paul's 8-year-old daughter, Olivia, had painted a blue sky, green grass with flowers, a green sun, and a white cross; on another side, his 6-year-old son, Nate, painted a vertical rainbow of colors. On the front, also in paint, were the small handprints of Olivia ("Livi"), Nate, and 18-month-old Luke. Inside the container were the ashes of their 44-year-old father, who had died after suffering a massive heart attack.

Paul's 37-year-old widow, Susan, decided to create a custom urn after visiting a funeral home and realizing that the traditional urns "weren't for me, weren't for Paul, and weren't for our kids. They looked too official, too old, and they didn't reflect our personalities," she explained. An art major in college, Susan went to an art supply store and bought a plain wooden box. Upon returning home, she told her two older children that they could each take one side of the box and paint whatever they wanted on it. On the top of the box, Susan wrote: "Brother, Son, Husband, Father, Friend. Paul Bryan Krahn."

Paul's heart attack had occurred after he returned home from work on a day when the weather begged everyone to be outdoors. Olivia and Nate were playing in the yard as Susan, her mother, and Susan's neighbor, watched them from the patio. After greeting everyone, Paul left for a short run. When he returned, he headed inside to clean up before getting ready to grill dinner for the group. Everything was normal—even idyllic. A short while later, the three women heard a loud thud. Rushing to the kitchen, they found Paul on the floor—he was obviously in pain and breathing heavily. Medics arrived at the house within minutes after 911 was called. Paul, who was treated on site, was then placed on a stretcher, and moved to an ambulance. "He was dead before we left for the hospital," Susan said.

While Susan was at the hospital with her husband's body, friends were caring for the couple's children. After

breakfast the next morning, Susan told Olivia and Nate that they wouldn't be going to school that day. Then she took the three children into the living room and said to them, "Dad went into the hospital, his heart was very sick and stopped working, and he's not with us any more." But she said she could tell that the youngsters didn't understand the ambiguity and wanted to know if their father was coming back. "No," Susan said, before uttering the weighty word she had hoped to avoid using with children so young, "he died." Then she added, "Dad's in heaven." Nate buried his head in the sofa and put his hands over his ears. "We were all crying," Susan said.

Several months after Paul's death, Olivia and her classmates were asked to draw their family as part of an in-school art project. Olivia had drawn four people: Susan, Olivia, Nate, and Luke; Paul wasn't in the picture. When Susan saw her daughter's drawing, she was crushed. She told Olivia that the drawing was beautiful, but then she disappeared into her bedroom where she wept over their loss. But the smiles on the faces in Olivia's drawing were very broad and bright, and the sky was very blue—when Susan finally noticed the joy in the picture, she reevaluated her daughter's work of art.

Around that same time, Olivia started asking Susan if she was going to remarry. Although Susan hadn't been dating (or thinking about doing so) she asked her daughter how she felt about the idea. "I think it would be great to have a man around the house so he can help us," was the young girl's response. Not giving up on the subject, Olivia—who inherited her mother's love of art—drew possible wedding dresses for Susan and periodically suggested potential honeymoon venues. Nate, too, expressed an interest in having a new father. He told his mom that he wanted someone who would mow their lawn and cut Nate's initials into the grass (as Paul used to do). She told Olivia and Nate, "I'm not ready to remarry. But maybe someday."

# Margaret
## Abdun-Nur

"While my kids are trying
to reach me at home
to see if I'm dead or alive,
I'm at Arthur Murray's
dancing the waltz with a
16-year-old boy."

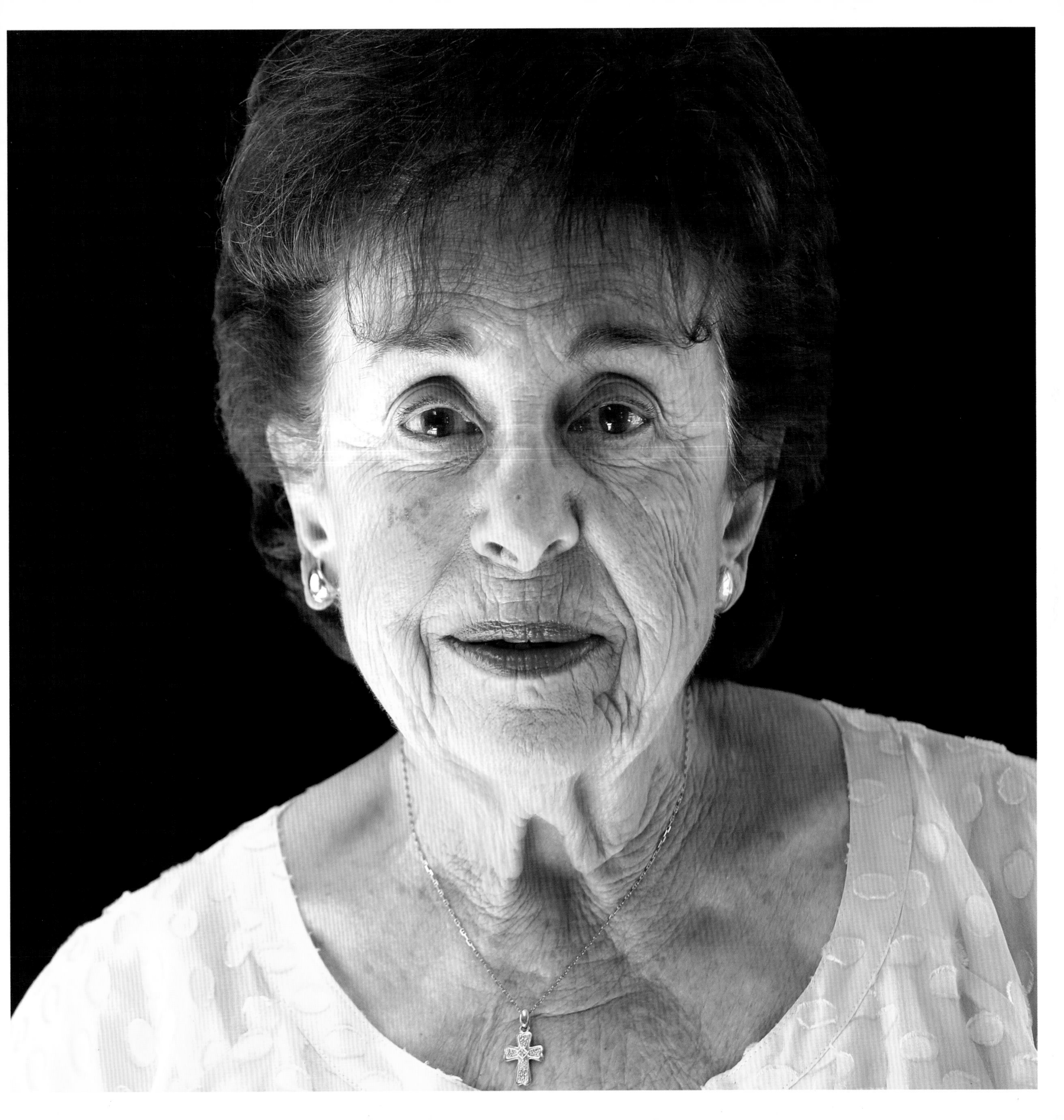

# Margaret Abdun-Nur

An hour and 30 minutes into their first date, just as the cheesecake was being served, John Abdun-Nur proposed to Margaret Haddad. A month later, the two were engaged. "It was love at first sight," Margaret said before adding: "He knew what he was looking for." And though only 18 at the time, Margaret acknowledged that she liked what she saw in John—someone who shared her values and was kind, gentle, and responsible. Her voice broke as she continued, "You couldn't help but love him."

Margaret and John, a physician, had been married for 59 years when John died of colon cancer. He had an earlier diagnosis (of rectal cancer) which had been treated by a painful surgical procedure. After six years of good health the cancer metastasized to his colon and, when it was obvious that his health had again changed, the doctor diagnosed himself and told no one—including his wife—about his condition.

"There's something about his generation..." Margaret said, her voice trailing off in thought. John, a gunnery officer in World War II, played football in school and grew up believing that men didn't cry. "He was strong," Margaret said. As a sudden smile illuminated her expression, she added, "He did things his way, like Frank Sinatra."

Months later, Margaret accidentally discovered the secret John had been concealing when she found blood in the toilet bowl. "I forced him to get in the car to see his doctor," she said. But when they arrived at the clinic, she couldn't convince him to talk with his physician or agree to an examination. Margaret recalled what John said at the time, "I'm a doctor and I'm going to do what I want to do." Her husband went on to explain that at the age of 83, he didn't want to prolong his life with additional harrowing treatments. Margaret, his practical and devoted wife, eventually relented.

Early in their marriage, when John was still involved in his busy and stressful medical practice, Margaret would tell their five children, "Dad's been dealing with people all day, so when he comes home give him hugs and kisses, but don't tell him about the fights you

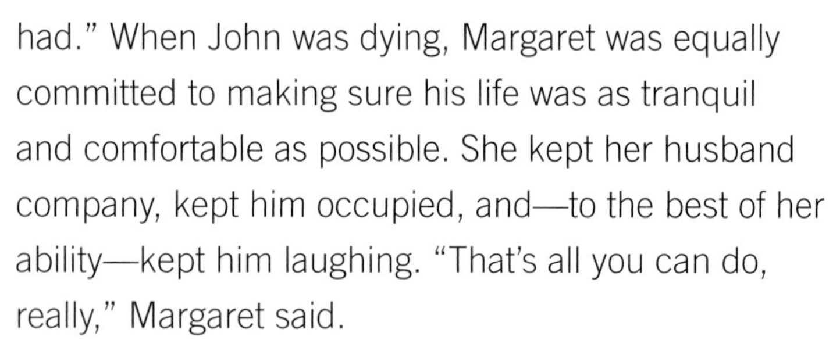

had." When John was dying, Margaret was equally committed to making sure his life was as tranquil and comfortable as possible. She kept her husband company, kept him occupied, and—to the best of her ability—kept him laughing. "That's all you can do, really," Margaret said.

The couple was alone in their home when John took his last breath. Margaret cried as she recalled her last words to him: "I love you forever. Take me with you."

She added, "We grew up together and when he died there was a huge void in my life. My kids kept telling me that I had to adjust." For a year after John's death, Margaret's grief was great and she suffered his loss deeply.

And then, one Christmas, her children gave her a gift certificate for dance lessons. "'Mom, you're always dancing in the kitchen,' they told me, 'go do some ballroom dancing.'" It was three months before

Margaret went to her first class and she's been moving to the music ever since. "I got hooked on ballroom dancing. And now my children complain that I'm never around," Margaret admitted with a laugh. "While my kids are trying to reach me at home to see if I'm dead or alive, I'm at Arthur Murray's dancing the waltz with a 16-year-old boy."

When Margaret turned 80, her children wanted to hold a birthday party in her honor. "It was a lovely thought," she said, "and they're all great cooks and love to bake, but their parties are boring as hell." So she told them that she would throw the party and that she (like her husband and Mr. Sinatra) would do it her way. "I hired a disc jockey," she said, "and served hot fudge sundaes for dessert instead of cake. And everyone danced."

# Octavio
## Cardona-Loya

“Oddly enough,
I still feel married
even though
I’ve been widowed
for more than
three years.”

# Octavio
## Cardona-Loya

Octavio Cardona-Loya was scrubbed, ready, and standing by in the operating room when his wife, Lissy, was declared dead. The previous morning, Lissy, who was 58, had told her plastic surgeon husband that her arm was hurting and she wasn't feeling well. While examining his wife, Octavio noticed that her pulse was abnormal and that her skin was cool to the touch. So he immediately called the hospital ER and told them he was bringing his spouse in. "She probably has a clot in her arm," Octavio recalled telling the person who was on the other end of the line. Lissy, who was a nurse when she and Octavio met, didn't want to go to the hospital. "Love cures all," she insisted. And then she repeated it in Spanish: "El amor cura todo."

But Lissy's protests were unsuccessful and, once at the hospital, she was given medication to dissolve her blood clot. The treatment was successful and everyone was relieved to learn that the clot in her arm had dissolved. The next morning, Lissy underwent a series of follow-up exams given by a team of specialists that included: a hematologist, vascular surgeon, primary care physician, and pulmonologist; pleased with her medical condition, the physicians gave her permission to walk around and receive visitors.

A relieved Lissy told Octavio (who had spent the night with her in the hospital) that she was fine and that he should go to his nearby office to catch up on work. She then asked their daughter, Michelle, who was also present, to get her some makeup so that she would look good when friends visited later in the day. Their son, Octavio Jr., remained in the room with his mother. A short while later, Lissy went to the bathroom and when she came out she told her son that she was having trouble breathing. After he alerted the nurses, a team of specialists hurried to Lissy's side and began resuscitative efforts.

Octavio, after receiving a frantic call from his son, ran back to the hospital. By that time, Lissy's physicians had determined that she had a pulmonary embolism and she was rushed into the operating room. Octavio, who had hospital privileges, was allowed to join her. Once there, surgeons opened her chest and removed the blood clot. But it was too late. Octavio touched his wife's heart—it was no longer beating. "The strange thing is that I was optimistic until the last minute," Octavio said. His eyes filled with tears as he recalled that awful day: "I didn't know how I was going to tell our kids that their mother had died."

The 64-year-old surgeon is emphatic: he doesn't plan to marry again. Neither is he interested in a serious relationship. "Oddly enough, I still feel married even though I've been widowed for more than three years. And that's the first thing I tell women who make advances." He grows quiet before adding in a barely audible voice, "I haven't gone to bed and awakened with someone next to me since my wife died. If I did, I would feel as though I were cheating on Lissy—physically—and on the other woman—mentally. I don't feel totally free." And then there are his adult children to consider; he doesn't believe they are ready to accept another woman in his life.

During their 33 years of marriage, Lissy and Octavio had occasional conversations about end-of-life issues. They agreed that the most important job of the surviving spouse would be to take care of their children. Family is very important to Octavio, and his is exceptionally close. Octavio Jr., 28, lives with his dad, and Melissa (who is a couple of years older than her brother and is married) resides 12 minutes away. Octavio spends weekends and holidays with his son, daughter, and son-in-law. Together, they try to fill the void Lissy's death left in all their lives.

# Kate
## Kerr Meigneux

"I was dealing with
a wide spectrum of emotions
and for every happy memory
there was a nightmare
that I couldn't shake."

# Kate
## Kerr Meigneux

"Everything about Patrice was larger than life," Kate said. "He was extremely attractive and had a seductive French accent. He loved to cook, enjoyed socializing, and always had something funny and provocative to say. But, before I met him, he had a long struggle with alcohol and cocaine abuse. Early in our relationship I thought it was manageable and that I could fix it."

But his addictions weren't manageable and, despite her efforts, Kate couldn't fix them. The couple underwent therapy. "There was something deep that Patrice couldn't, or wouldn't, allow anyone to reach," Kate said. "He could be honest up to a point—then he would just close down. He lived a life that was very compartmentalized, although I don't think I realized that at the time."

Four different friends had introduced the couple to each other, separately, none aware that the others also wanted to connect Kate and Patrice. Each friend had independently come to the conclusion that the talented and good-looking designer from London, Kate Kerr, and the talented and good-looking photographer from France, Patrice Meigneux, belonged together. After their four arranged dates, the pair agreed that they were, indeed, well matched. They moved in together and, five years later, they were wed.

Kate continued to work as a designer, but she also developed a passion for Japanese Taiko drumming and joined a touring ensemble. Ten years after she and Patrice were married, while she was with the ensemble on a two-week tour of the Hawaiian Islands, Patrice called to tell her he had suffered a heart attack and was being driven to the hospital by a friend. The next time they spoke, Patrice had undergone triple bypass surgery. "I can fly home immediately," Kate offered, but both her husband and his doctor assured her that there was no need. When she later called the hospital for an update, Kate was refused information about her husband's condition; Patrice had authorized the delivery of particulars about his health to only one person. And that person was his girlfriend. That was when—and how—Kate learned that there was another woman in her husband's life.

After his release from the hospital, Patrice went directly to the home of a male friend to recuperate—he was unable to climb the stairs at the loft home he and his wife shared with their 8 and 10-year-old daughters. Kate, just back from Hawaii, gathered the girls and went to see him. "I could tell that he wanted to say something to me, but our children were present and there wasn't an opportunity," she said.

When Kate went to visit Patrice the following night, she entered a scene full of confusion and noise. Police and personnel from the coroner's office seemed to fill the bedroom Patrice had been staying in. His girlfriend, newly emboldened, was crying loudly in the next room. Patrice's 55-year-old body had given out and was encased in a thick, plastic bag and ready for transport. "That evening I was robbed of the chance to say a quiet goodbye to Patrice. And that's haunted me," Kate said.

Shortly after his death, Kate discovered photographs of Patrice and his girlfriend—evidence that the affair had been going on for more than a decade. She also learned that close friends were aware of the relationship. Kate felt betrayed and was left questioning everything, including herself. Her sense of loss—and loss of face—almost overwhelmed her.

"I was dealing with a wide spectrum of emotions and for every happy memory there was a nightmare that I couldn't shake. I was second-guessing things that I had previously taken for granted and revisiting assumptions about love and respect."

Kate and her daughters began the process of recovery with a trip to visit friends and family in England and France. When they returned home, Kate was welcomed by her Buddhist community and warmly embraced by clients who had kept their design projects on hold while she was healing. Surrounded by people who loved and comforted her, and after a long period of introspection and reflection, Kate began to regain her confidence. "I slowly rebuilt my life," she said.

Early in their courtship, Kate and Patrice had occasional dinners with a married couple, Adam and Jill, with whom they shared mutual friends and similar career interests. The couples lived in different parts of the city, though, and eventually drifted apart. Three years after Patrice's death, Adam placed an unexpected and unsettling call to Kate to tell her that Jill was in the hospital with complications from gallbladder surgery and wasn't likely to survive. Adam knew that Kate would understand what it was like to experience a young spouse's swift and fatal decline in health. During the emotional turmoil and grief surrounding his wife's death, Kate supported and counseled her old friend. Five months later, Kate and Adam became a couple—they share their lives, and studio space, with a handsome puppy and Kate's two mature and charming teenagers. "I trust Adam," a smiling Kate said, "absolutely."

# Lydia
## Lewis

"It's because of my
personal experiences
that I've really come
to understand death as a
continuum of life."

# Lydia Lewis

"I saw my husband, Reggie, on the floor of our living room," Lydia Lewis recalled. "I thought he was doing yoga stretches, but I didn't see a mat and wondered why he'd be exercising on the hardwood floor. Then I realized that his arm was positioned in an awkward and strange manner..." It was at this point that Lydia, who couldn't lift her fallen spouse on her own, dialed 911. "Reggie pleaded with me not to call," Lydia said, "because that would mean something was seriously wrong. But something was seriously wrong." Reggie had just suffered a stroke.

A practicing psychotherapist, Lydia said that she is usually able to remain focused and controlled during a crisis. "But I became frantic in the ER," she said. "The scene was chaotic and the staff had trouble locating my husband. Most of that evening was a blur; but I did know that the prognosis was bad and that Reggie was going to lose the quality of life he had treasured and counted on." The couple met when Lydia was 32 and Reggie was 48. She was at the start of her career and he had recently retired from his job as a chief detective in the New York Police Department. In search of a leisurely lifestyle, Reggie veered from chasing bad guys to painting, reading, cooking, and managing the couple's household. He also introduced into their world people whom his wife, who had lived a fairly sheltered and protected life, never thought she'd meet. One such person was a Mafia Don who wanted Reggie to escort him to and from court appearances because he trusted the retired detective's integrity. Lydia understood that trust. "Reggie did exactly what he said he was going to do...when he said he was going to do it." It was one of the many things she loved about her husband.

Almost 20 years into their marriage, Reggie was diagnosed with prostate cancer. After treatment by Western and Eastern doctors, his disease went into remission. Fifteen years later—while he was in the hospital recovering from his stroke—the couple learned that the prostate cancer had returned. Reggie spent most of the remaining nine months of his life at a rehabilitation center. The formerly vigorous man began to decline; he grew thin and frail, his memory started to fail, and he had difficulty speaking.

Lydia continued to work, and she created a schedule so that Reggie was never alone when she was seeing clients. She hired one of her husband's closest friends to be his primary caregiver. "My husband could tell him to 'Go to hell,'" she said, "and he wouldn't be insulted or take it personally." And Reggie's son from his first marriage flew across the country to help care for his father. Lydia's best friend came and helped, as well. And Lydia spent quiet evenings and weekends with Reggie. But she never stopped working. She was helping others deal with loss as she, herself, was struggling to keep her feelings at bay. "This is how I avoid pain," she said with a shrug of resignation. "I work."

After Reggie died, Lydia added more hours to her office schedule. She exhausted herself and rarely spent time at home. It took more than a year for Lydia to realize that she was too tired to continue at that pace. And when she allowed herself to slow down, her longing for Reggie increased. As part of her work as a therapist, Lydia helps clients understand and explore the stages of grief; it's what she was educated and trained to do. "But," she said, "it's because of my personal experiences that I've really come to understand death as a continuum of life." Lydia, whose grandparents, parents, siblings, and husband are all deceased, said. "I believe protracted grief is unhealthy and doesn't allow the 'spirit' of the dead to be free. I make every effort to release my hold on those who have died."

# Jack
## Fleck

"Staying single after
the death of my first wife
wasn't an option.
I didn't like coming home
to an empty house
and I wanted
to share my life again."

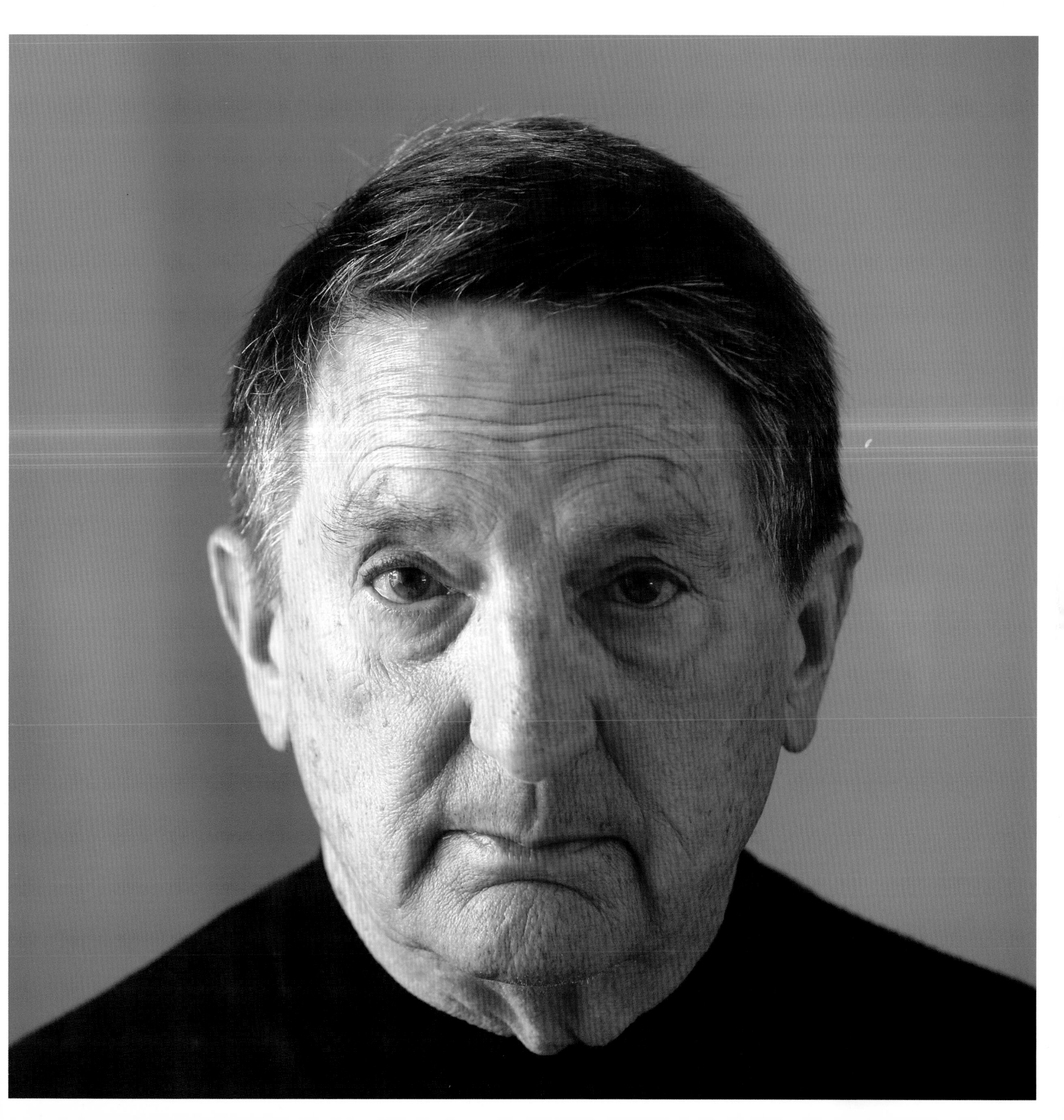

# Jack
## Fleck

Six months after meeting Deborah LeDoux on an online dating site, Jack Fleck invited her to join him at an event in Las Vegas. While in their large hotel suite, Jack handed Deborah a letter. The emotions and words expressed in it had come easily to him, but he edited and tweaked the text over several days before presenting his written declaration of love. The letter read, in part:

"Honey, you are the center of my universe and I have never been surer of myself when I say that I want you in my life forever."

Jack followed the moment by revealing a box that he had previously hidden in their room. Tucked inside was a diamond ring. "And then," he said, "we both started to cry."

A year earlier, Jack was widowed when his first wife, Ginny, succumbed to breast cancer. "I was attracted to Ginny the first time I saw her," Jack recalled. "We met in the laundry room of our apartment complex and married a few months later."

The couple, who spent 47 years together and were parents to four sons, built a strong and devoted family unit.

Seven years after her original cancer diagnosis, Ginny was informed that the disease had metastasized to her lungs and liver. "We became even closer," Jack said. "Ginny—who had a gentle, compassionate, and humorous nature—was stoic throughout her illness. No tears and no drama. She tried to spare her family the burdens she carried internally." Aware of the probability that Ginny had only a few years before the cancer would take her life, Jack cut back on his work schedule to spend more time with his wife—and then he quit his job to become her full-time caregiver when her condition grew worse.

Ginny died at home with her husband lying next to her in bed. "I was absolutely devastated," Jack said of his wife's death, "but I was also at peace with myself because I knew that I had done everything I possibly could to make sure she was comfortable and pain free."

Jack was aware that he would always mourn the loss of Ginny, but he also believed that the intensity of his grief would lessen and knew that he would want to find a relationship to fill the void in his world. "Staying single after the death of my first wife wasn't an option. I didn't like coming home to an empty house and I wanted to share my life again."

After almost five decades of marriage, Jack had several concerns about dating. He recalled his teenage years when there were the people who were dumped and those who did the dumping. "A few times I was the one who was dumped," Jack remembered. He didn't know what the current singles scene was like and worried that "all the good

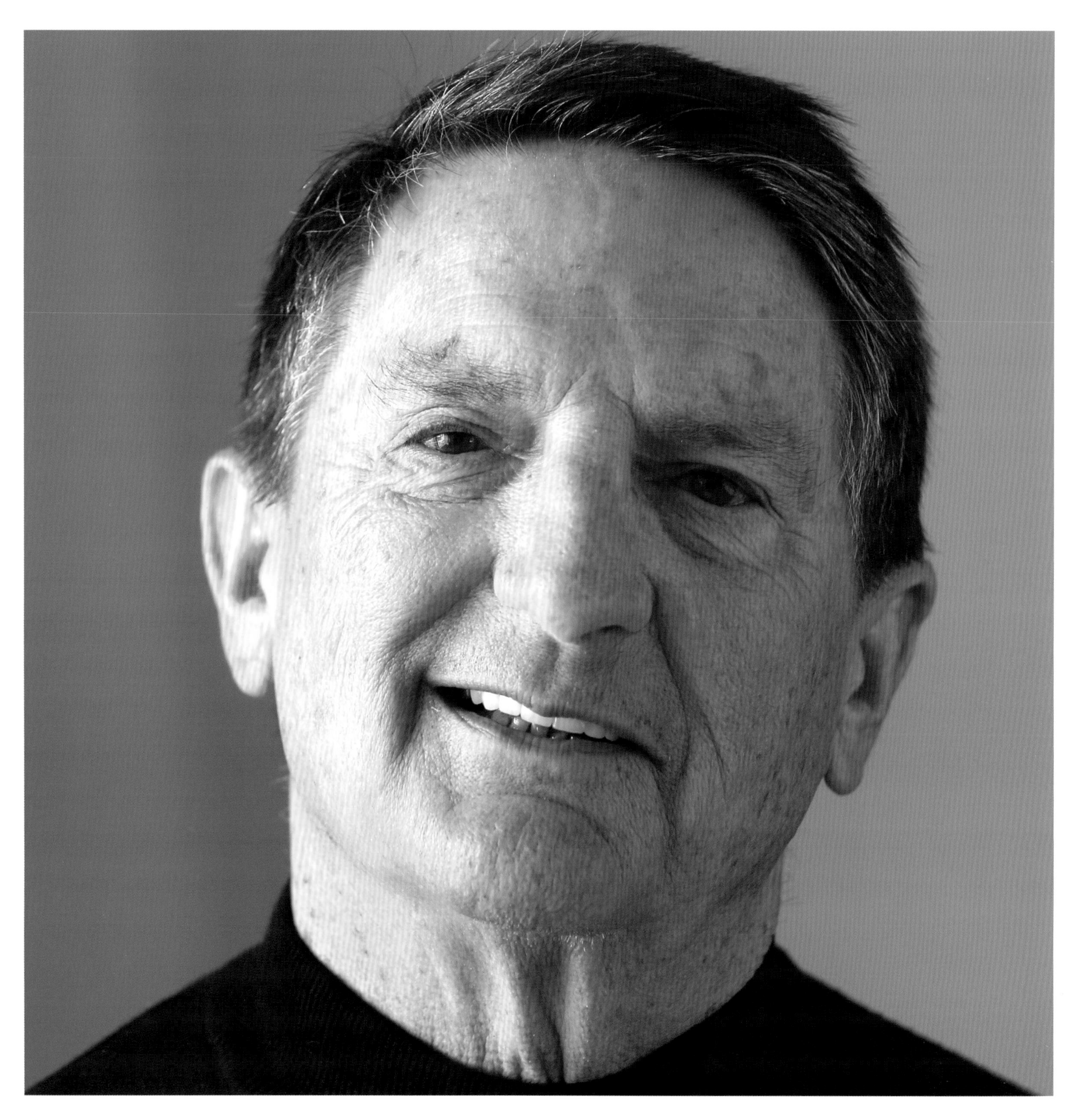

women were probably taken." Although eager to find someone to spend the rest of his life with, Jack said he wasn't willing to settle nor was he comfortable conducting his search in bars or clubs. After hearing about "eHarmony" he decided to give online dating a try.

Almost immediately after his profile was posted, Jack was notified that he had more than 150 possible matches. "I had to set up a spread sheet to keep them straight," he said laughing. And while Jack enjoyed getting to know new women, he was looking for something serious. So, if on the first date he saw signs that the relationship wasn't going to lead to marriage—there wasn't a second meeting.

Jack dated almost 20 women before he came across Deborah's profile and read that her first marriage had been happy and that she, too, was widowed and wanted to remarry. In fact, he liked everything about Deborah's profile. His interest and anticipation were only heightened by the subsequent wide-ranging and candid phone conversations he had with her.

On the drive home from his first date with Deborah, Jack phoned one of his sons and told him, "My quest is over. I found my woman."

# Deborah
## Fleck

"I wanted to be a wife again;
I was a good wife.
And I wanted another
happy marriage."

# Deborah Fleck

Deborah Fleck found herself in a strange and frightening new world after her first husband, Jim LeDoux, died—and she didn't know how to navigate within it. A successful and focused business owner before his death, she became disengaged and uncertain after it.

Searching for a way to return—somehow—to the life she knew and the man she missed, Deborah decided to attend an event led by a well-known psychic medium. "I became very caught up in trying to contact Jim's spirit," she said. "I was sitting in the audience praying that Jim was present and trying to communicate with me. I was desperate to be with my husband again and I knew I was close to becoming obsessed." Deborah also interrogated and tortured herself with questions: had she gotten Jim to a doctor soon enough; had she had done everything she could for Jim after he received a diagnosis of Stage IV non-Hodgkin's lymphoma; had she comforted him enough; had she made the right decisions towards the end of his life? She was experiencing guilt and grief and struggling to find a way to deal with her intense emotions.

In desperation, Deborah turned to a grief counselor who believed that the 54-year-old widow would benefit from attending a bereavement support group. "I was afraid to go," Deborah said. "I thought the room would be filled with a bunch of old widows. And I didn't want to be an old widow; I didn't want to be in a room full of people whose lives were over. But I was wrong about the women and I was wrong about the experience. Joining the support group helped me a great deal." In addition to finding comfort and solace among people who understood her roiling emotions, Deborah was also introduced to nurturing rituals and tools that helped her start healing. She started a journal, lit a candle nightly, meditated—she learned that she could cry and that the tears wouldn't overtake her days or her life.

A year and a half after Jim's death, Deborah—whose business eventually dwindled to nothing without her leadership—found a fulfilling job, took control of her finances, and her confidence started to grow again. "I was content on my own," she said. "I had a structured life that made me happy, I had a great job at which I was successful, I had a condo and a cat. But I wanted to be a wife again; I was a good wife. And I wanted another happy marriage." So she started dating. "I became involved in a couple of long term relationships with men who wanted to get married. But I didn't want to marry them," Deborah said firmly. "I wanted someone who really had his shit together—whose character was strong and who was smart, had a great sense of humor, and was loving and fun to be with. I wanted someone I could admire."

In her profile for the online dating site, "eHarmony," Deborah wrote honestly about her desire for a long-term relationship that would lead to marriage. She received roughly 30 potential matches one of which led to Jack Fleck, a widower who stated he had been happily married. Deborah—intrigued—responded. In the first stage of their courtship, Jack and Deborah answered a variety of questions posed by their Internet matchmaker. Their interest in each other increased as the process proceeded and the questions, and their answers, became more complex and personal. As their comfort level grew, they added lengthy phone conversations to the mix and, finally, the couple progressed to a face-to-face meeting. After many hours of conversation and occasional hand-holding, each was confident

that their search had ended. "I remember saying to myself, 'I don't want to miss a word this man has to say,'" Deborah said. "He just took my breath away. I knew I had found the man I was going to marry."

Six months after they met, Deborah and Jack were wed. "I've not always chosen my dates wisely," said Deborah, "but I was very careful about the men I married."

# Ken
## Fousel

"I was a 'macho,
I-can-do-it-by-myself-and-
I-don't-need-any-help'
kind of guy until I became
my wife's caregiver."

# Ken
## Fousel

Ken Fousel knows that for many men talking openly about their feelings can be difficult. He, however, isn't one of those men—not anymore. "I used to say I could cut off my left arm with my right hand and not cry about it," Ken said as he forcefully drove his right hand across his left arm to demonstrate. "I was a 'macho, I-can-do-it-by-myself-and-I-don't-need-any-help' kind of guy until I became my wife's caregiver."

Ken's wife, Liz, was diagnosed with Alzheimer's when she was 60 years old; she died 19 years later. During that lengthy illness, Ken realized two important things: he couldn't do everything by himself and he couldn't cure his wife's disease. So this retired, career military officer tried to manage by learning everything he could about Alzheimer's from the experts. After absorbing as much information as possible, he decided to share what he had learned with other caregivers. As he traveled from support group to support group, cofacilitating meetings and talking about his experiences, Ken was struck by how the men shut down their emotions while the women opened up.

"Women are much more social and better able to communicate their feelings freely. Men are cultured to be stoic and reserved," he said. The men he encountered at the support groups were used to being "fixers and problem solvers." They went there to get help, according to Ken, but weren't comfortable being viewed as vulnerable and overwhelmed—especially in front of women. Ken, being a fixer and problem solver himself, set out to do something about that.

In 1998 he started a men's only support group with the assistance of California's Southern Caregiver Resource Center. Ken's tone turned to that of group facilitator when he said, "Let me tell you how things typically unfold at our meetings. The first time a man shows up, he sits silently like this," and he crossed his arms protectively across his chest. "At the second meeting he responds to questions. And at the third meeting you'd better have tissues ready because he becomes unhinged. It takes two meetings for him to recover; from then on he is 100 percent in the game." Support is something Ken still needs for himself, now more than ever. He cared for his wife at home for 11 years until she had a series of strokes and eventually became paralyzed. Following an episode of acute pancreatitis, Liz became psychotic and was moved to a facility. As his wife's condition worsened, Ken became friends—and then close friends—with Lynne, a woman in one of his support groups whose husband soon died. "Lynne and I were very concerned that we would get involved too soon because of our loneliness," Ken recalled. "So we deliberately kept each other at arms length and didn't allow ourselves to become emotionally attached. Or so we thought." But they fell in love and moved in with each other in 2002.

On June 20, 2008, Lynne was diagnosed with Frontotemporal Dementia; eight days later Ken's wife, Liz, died. Two years later Lynne, had a psychotic episode after getting a urinary tract infection and was rushed to a hospital. Now Ken was Lynne's caregiver. She never returned to the couple's home—moving instead to the same full care facility in which Liz had lived.

As Ken talks about Lynne's decline and the fact that she no longer recognizes him, he tears up for the first time in our conversation. "I speak to her, not with her. She's unresponsive," he said as his voice broke. "It's an odd thing, but I'm having much more difficulty losing Lynne than Liz. The second time around you'd think it would be easier."

"When I lost my wife, I still had a very bright future ahead of me…now I don't," Ken said. The 82-year-old continued, "I'm having a more difficult time regaining my enthusiasm for life." Ken, who identifies himself as being a problem solver, was quick to add that he has regularly scheduled appointments with a psychologist and is actively working on making his life better. "I've turned a page and I'm in the middle of redefining myself." And—if he needs help—he has a group of friends he can turn to for support.

# Susan

## Levy

"Our family turned to me
for answers and direction;
I was 28 years old and
I thought I had answers,
but I didn't."

# Susan
## Levy

It was an early morning the week before Thanksgiving in 1978 when Chuck Netzer kissed his wife Susan goodbye and walked quietly past the bedrooms where his 6-week-old son was sleeping in his crib and his two-year-old daughter was asleep in her bed. He closed the front door, got into his car, and headed to his office. An hour later Susan received the phone call that would signal the end of the life she had been living—Chuck had been in a car accident and was in the operating room at a nearby hospital. Confused and in shock, Susan found someone to care for her children and rushed to be with her husband. When Chuck's surgery was over, he was moved to intensive care and hooked up to a mechanical ventilator. Susan's 29-year-old husband was brain-dead.

The couple, who had been married for eight years, had never talked about end-of-life issues.

"Our family turned to me for answers and direction; I was 28 years old and I thought I had answers, but I didn't," said Susan. "Until the doctors officially announced that Chuck was brain-dead and should be removed from life support, I kept thinking that he would snap out of it," she said, "and that a miracle would occur."

Once Susan was able to accept the finality of the situation and understood that Chuck wouldn't be able to breathe without the aid of the ventilator, she agreed to have it disconnected. "But first, I kissed him goodbye and told him that I loved him and that he would be with God." She left his hospital room before he took his last breath. "I decided I couldn't be there at that moment…looking back, I wish I had been," she said as she shed tears for her first love. "Not an hour in the day goes by when I don't think of him."

Though she knew that she wasn't to blame, Susan felt guilty that her children would grow up without their father. She was also very angry about the enormous loss in her life and felt overwhelmed by a sense of abandonment. This wasn't the first time Susan had experienced such heavy emotional turmoil, though. When she was 13 years old, her mother walked out on her family, leaving nothing but a note behind. Six years later, Susan's father died. With Chuck's death, she was once again faced with an empty chair at her kitchen table.

Within a short time, however, that chair was filled. Bryan Levy was the 21-year-old son of Susan's closest friends. She had known Bryan for several years, but he had become a frequent presence in her life—and the lives of her children—after Chuck's death. "It was easy to talk with him; everything was easy between us," Susan said. After a few months of platonic interaction, Bryan asked Susan to join him for an evening out. "We started dating and it was a whirlwind," she said. "No one before Bryan had ever treated me romantically—brought me an unexpected bouquet of flowers, or jewelry, or made an effort to please and court me."

Despite initial—and strong—protests from his parents, the couple married a little more than a year after Chuck's death. They had a son, but within five years Bryan had become withdrawn and inattentive and the couple divorced, only to marry each other again two years later. And this time they stayed married for 15 years. However, once they settled into a routine Bryan again seemed distant and depressed, and the pair sought counseling. Confused and concerned, Susan eventually confronted her husband and asked him if he was having an affair. It was then that he told her he was gay. It was a week after her mother, with whom she had reconciled, died. Susan was once more in mourning. "I was grieving the loss of my mother, my husband, and my world as I thought I knew it," she said.

Six years after her divorce, Susan bought a new home with her then pregnant daughter and son-in-law. Sitting in a living room surrounded by walls lined with family photographs and an orderly arrangement of toys for the now four-year-old twins, Susan—the principal of a suburban middle school—said, "My grandchildren are my world now, and my life is good." Susan paused, smiled, and then added, "I've become the person I was meant to be. I can do anything that I want to do now. I'm no longer afraid."

# Aaron
## Borovoy

"When a couple has been together for a long time, there are three entities. There's a 'you,' a 'me,' and an 'us.'"

# Aaron
## Borovoy

As he scattered his husband's ashes from the Golden Gate Bridge, the song "Light Sings" by the Fifth Dimension started randomly playing on Aaron Borovoy's iPod. The music was appropriate to the occasion and the opening lyrics brought him to tears: "The sun comes up / The moon goes down / A new day's on its way."

In many ways, Aaron's life was starting over. He had been with John Laird since they met at a bar in 1983. "There wasn't an immediate physical attraction between us," Aaron said, "but there was something else—an interesting connection—and we became friends. Shortly after that, our friendship developed into a significant relationship." Smiling, he added: "We complemented each other very well. He was 35, ex-military, a father of two, and the most gregarious person I'd ever met; I was 22 and a shy word processing operator. He loved being in the spotlight and I was more comfortable working behind the scenes. Eventually, we both became interested in philanthropy and worked as a team in my reform synagogue and our local LGBT Center. If it weren't for John and his influence, I never would have gained the confidence to be who I am now. Everything I learned about functioning in a larger society, I learned from him."

Aaron and John married in July 2008 during the brief time when same-sex marriage was legal in California. Five years into their relationship, John was diagnosed with Type 2 diabetes. According to Aaron, genetics and smoking contributed to the condition; John's weight and failure to follow his doctor's recommendations further affected his health. Aaron knew that John wouldn't listen to his advice, either. But, after John was in intensive care in an induced coma, Aaron did give his husband one ultimatum: stop smoking. "If you pick up one more cigarette, I'm out the door," Aaron told him. John never touched another cigarette. But it was too late, and when John collapsed on his way to a meeting they learned he also had congestive heart failure. He was in and out of the hospital for several years and survived numerous procedures, but his health continued to decline.

When John needed care, Aaron defined himself as a "supportive spouse" rather than a "caregiver." The first time Aaron was a caregiver he was in his teens; he was the only child of a divorced mother who was chronically ill and died at the age of 51. Neither John nor Aaron wanted him to take on that mantle for a second time. Aaron didn't acknowledge that he was, in fact, a caregiver until it was clear that John wasn't going to survive his last illness. At that point, Aaron was reconciled to the role and knew he had the experience and commitment to care for his husband.

Aaron also tried to provide social stimulation for John, an extroverted man who was confined to his apartment with a television and phone for company. The situation wasn't without conflict, guilt and occasional anger. During the day Aaron was busy at work; at night, as the new president of his congregation, he was occupied with meetings. "Handling him became a full-time job and was emotionally exhausting," Aaron recalled. "But I wouldn't change it for the world," he quickly added.

When John died, his 50-year-old widower "got the sick out of the house"—he removed the adjustable hospital bed and related paraphernalia—and started living his life without John. There were practical financial matters to consider, so Aaron found a roommate to share his two-bedroom townhouse. He gave her the master bedroom and moved into the spare. "In some ways, that was another death…moving from our space into my space. My first evening in my new bedroom, I cried all night," Aaron said.

He also decided to grow the beard John would have hated. "Not only did I like it," he said, "but it gave me new confidence. I also bought new clothes and, when the insurance money came in, I got a new car. The car I wanted, not the car he wanted. The car we had was boring," he laughed. And, in time, he started dating. But he still misses John. "When a couple has been together for a long time," Aaron said, "there are three entities. There's a 'you,' a 'me,' and an 'us.' I miss John," Aaron continued, "but I miss 'us' even more."

# Fanny
## Shwartz

"He didn't feel foreign to me—
he felt like family.
I knew what I was getting into."

# Fanny Shwartz

A four-foot-something redhead, who refers to herself as "one of the ancients," was exiting a popular restaurant in Los Angeles when someone called her name: "Fanny, Fanny Shwartz." A woman with a familiar face and voice was waving at her. Cynthia Nixon, the award-winning actor and star of "Sex in the City," hadn't seen Fanny in a while and wanted to catch up. That's the kind of person Fanny is: people who know her—even famous people—love her. Fanny is celebrated for her wit, self-deprecating style, and light-hearted (but intelligent) conversation. She is also someone who has known tragedy in her 90 years.

In Judaism, when a relative dies, the immediate family might practice a ritual called "sitting shiva." During this time, mourners assemble for a week to celebrate the life of the deceased and receive visitors who gather to comfort them. Five days after the death of her mother, Fanny and her husband, Sam Silverman, who had turned 45 years old earlier that week, were sitting shiva with family and friends when Sam suffered a heart attack and died.

Fanny and Sam had been friends since elementary school; he had been her date for the senior prom. "We didn't think of not getting married," Fanny said. "It was inevitable." The young couple had two daughters and worked hard (as did many of their friends and neighbors) to maintain a lower middle class lifestyle. They also went out dancing as often as they could—wherever there was no cover charge.

After Sam's sudden death, it was up to Fanny to financially support her family. Over the next several decades she held many jobs: high school English teacher, financial aid manager, tutor to non-English speakers, and administrator at a legal-aid society. "I never thought of any of these jobs as careers," said Fanny, "and I regret hopping around as often as I did." But she was always able to find a way to earn money and to keep her mind engaged. One of Fanny's most unique assignments was with a wealthy investor for whom she worked 15 minutes a day, five days a week. She spent those 15 minutes calling clients around the world and filling them in on financial information gathered during time differences between financial centers. It was in the pre-Internet days and she was paid a dollar a minute. But her favorite role was that of tutor for a blind UCLA student. Fanny helped the young woman prepare for exams, read to her, and drove her to various appointments. Fanny's sense of direction, however, was so bad that the unsighted woman ended up navigating as they drove around L.A. Though decades apart in age, the pair became close friends.

Eight years after her first husband died, Fanny met Puggy Shwartz, the nephew of her brother-in-law; Puggy was also widowed. He asked Fanny to marry him four days after they met. Ten days later, she did. "Over the years, Puggy and I had heard a lot about each other from various relatives. He didn't feel foreign to me—he felt like family. I knew what I was getting into," she said. One of the things Fanny knew she was getting into was marriage to a man with a history of heart problems.

One night, 13 years into their marriage, Fanny and Puggy went to dinner with another couple. In the middle of their meal, Puggy put down his drink and quietly slipped to the floor. A crowd surrounded them and someone tried to resuscitate her husband while someone else called 911. It was 20 minutes before the ambulance arrived and the EMTs declared Puggy dead; he'd suffered a heart attack.

There were a number of losses and challenges in Fanny's life—she grew up during the Great Depression and had parents who escaped the pogroms of central Europe—so she is philosophical about both the challenges and gifts that come with being alive. "My husbands died—everyone dies. And their lives, and deaths, are part of my life but not the sum total. Many things, major and minor, make up my memories and fill my days."

Although Fanny can't do everything she could a few years ago (such as square dancing with friends—which she did until the age of 86), the spark that attracts people is still present. Whether she's traveling to visit her older daughter in Santa Fe, camping with her younger daughter in Canada, or walking around Santa Monica (where she still lives independently) people, young and old, seek her company; some even wave and call her name.

# Roswitha
## Enright

"I would have found
a way to help him die.
I promised him
and I wanted to keep
my promise."

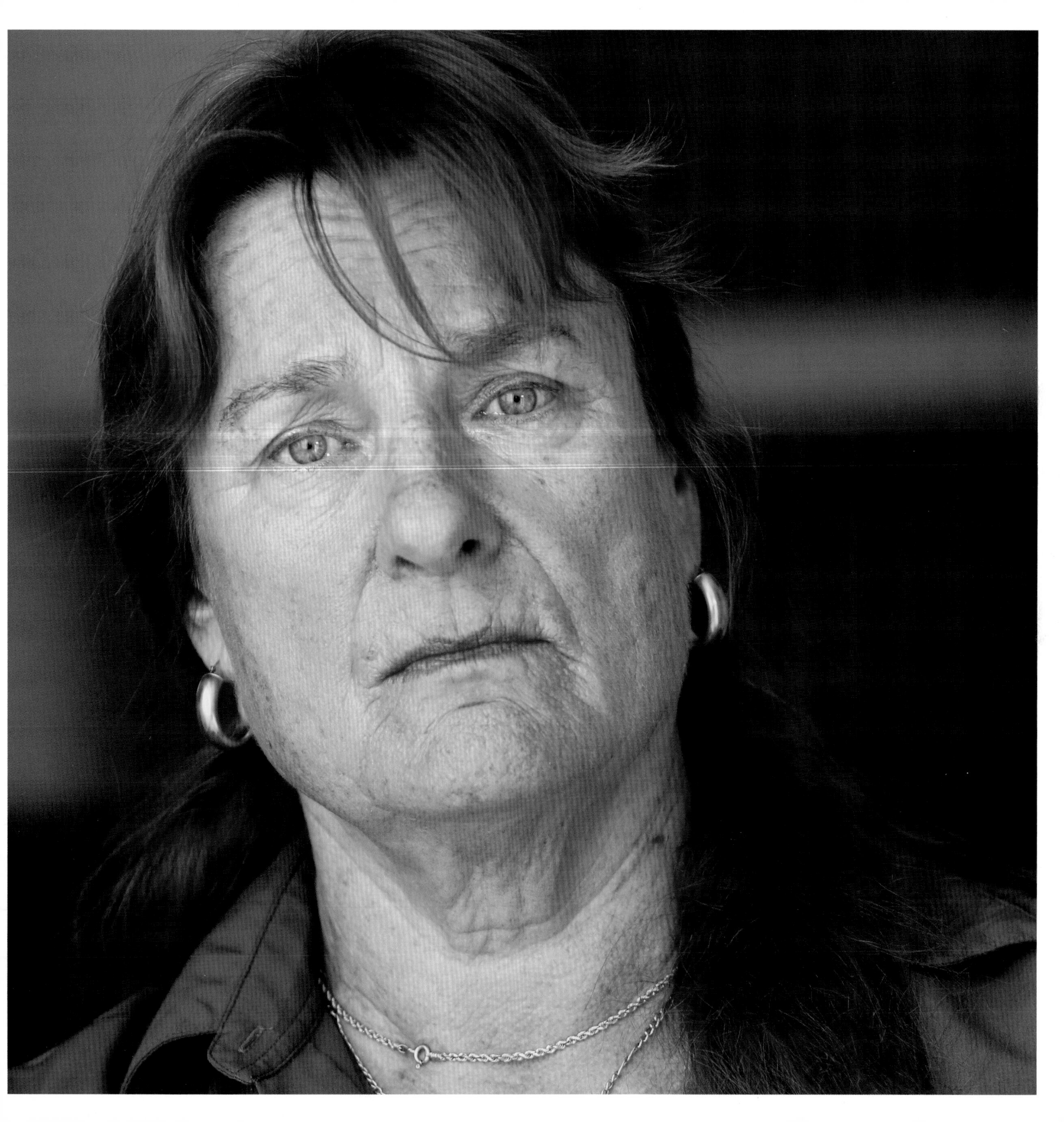

# Roswitha Enright

In 1998, Roswitha Enright wrote the following:

"To Whom It May Concern,

For many years I have held the conviction that one should be allowed to end one's life if it does not seem worth living anymore due to physical or mental illness. I hope I will be able to take care of my self-deliverance. Should I be unable to do so, it is my absolute wish that my spouse or another person very close to me will help me achieve my goal and give me a peaceful and quick death."

Roswitha's husband, Jim Enright, wrote a similar declaration. The letters were formal confirmation of verbal commitments the couple had made to each other when they were still young and healthy—a time when a conversation about euthanasia might be considered theoretical.

The couple met in 1966 when Roswitha, still living and working in her native Germany, was hired to work as Jim's lab assistant at a prestigious research institution in the United States. Her employment was sight unseen, but Roswitha said that there was an immediate attraction when she and Jim met. Two years later the pair were married. "He was the center of my life, my one great love, my teacher, my pupil. He needed me just like I needed him. We were totally happy just to be with one another," Roswitha said.

After almost three decades of marriage, Roswitha started noticing changes in Jim that worried her. "He wasn't his normal self; he wasn't as logical as he used to be," she said, "but when I questioned him about it he told me not to worry, he said he was just getting old." Her husband, at the time, was 65.

Worry escalated to panic when Jim went missing while he was in Florida to attend an annual conference. Roswitha was vacationing on Bainbridge Island at the time, and Jim promised to call her when he arrived at the motel he had stayed at on previous trips. When she didn't hear from him, Roswitha called the motel and learned that he hadn't checked in. After contacting hospitals and the rental car company, she was in the process of considering flying to Florida when the motel manager finally called: her husband was found—sound asleep—in an empty room in the motel. It was 48 hours since Jim had landed in Florida and he was unable to remember anything that occurred during that time.

Within a few weeks, Jim was diagnosed with dementia. That's when he and his wife each reiterated, in writing, their wish for a death that was free of suffering and pain.

Jim's illness progressed quickly and he no longer responded to things that had given him pleasure in the past—such as the sight of the ocean and his wife's kiss. Jim's movements became labored, the few words he spoke made no sense, he was incontinent, and swallowing was challenging for him. Roswitha knew she needed immediate practical advice if she was going to honor the promise she made to her husband to help him find an easy death if he couldn't do so for himself.

So she spoke with an attorney, with a friend in Holland who was a cardiologist, and with a friend in Berlin who had helped her own husband die when he was suffering with advanced cancer. She even attempted a veiled conversation about euthanasia with her husband's physician. They were all sympathetic, but no one could, or would, help her.

On September 22, 2004, Jim developed complications as a result of his rare form of neurodegenerative disease; he had a fever and trouble breathing. He was at home, as he had been throughout his illness, and Roswitha gave him some Tylenol and tried to make him comfortable. And then she called a hospice for help, but they needed a physician's referral before they could provide assistance. Roswitha then called Jim's doctor but was unable to reach him. At that point she was distraught, exhausted, and unable to think properly so—after talking with their son—she took a Valium and went to bed. When she woke up, Jim was dead.

Even though Jim died without assistance, Roswitha still believes emphatically in the commitment they made to each other. "I would have found a way to help him die," she said. "I promised him and I wanted to keep my promise."

# Renee
## Aragon

"When I was escorted to the ER, I saw officers lined up behind the captain and they were all standing at attention. Tears were streaming down their faces."

# Renee

## Aragon

Renee Aragon occasionally slips into the present tense when talking about her late husband, Ken. She misses him and loves him, but remains mindful that their married life was complex and often challenging. Although Renee and Ken had five children together, and shared a desire to keep their family intact and their union from unraveling, Ken's uncontrolled drinking ultimately destroyed their relationship and resulted in his death at the age of 47.

Their life together began on a very different note: the couple met at a singles event held by a Christian ministry. "I was attracted to his sweet disposition," Renee said. "He was reserved and humble and had a gentleness about him that was endearing. He was also a very good-looking guy," she said as she flashed a bright smile and drew attention to the photographs of Ken that sat on surfaces around the room.

Ken was a military policeman in the Marine Corps when he and Renee married. Within a year, he left the military and joined their local police force. It was after the birth of the couple's first child that Renee began to see signs that her marriage was far from the one she had initially imagined. Ken had begun drinking and staying out late with colleagues on the force. And rather than spending his pay on necessities for the family, he was buying expensive toys for himself. In a short period of time, he had purchased a motorcycle, an RV, and an array of fishing equipment. To help support their growing family and to prepare for a future that now appeared uncertain, Renee got a job outside her home. But she did so reluctantly—her mother had been a stay-at-home mom and she hoped to be one as well.

As part of her ongoing effort to keep her family together, Renee tried to focus on the aspects of her husband's character that she loved and respected. "He was an adoring, demonstrative, and playful father," she said, "and Ken gave generously to causes without expecting anything in return. He was also good at his job and genuinely committed to the community he served."

As time went on, though, it became increasingly difficult for the young mother to stay positive. Renee said that Ken's conduct, despite several attempts at marriage counseling, continued to disappoint and anger her. The turning point occurred one evening when Ken came home excessively intoxicated and the couple's children became involuntary witnesses to their father's disintegration and collapse. After that incident, Renee hired a lawyer and divorce papers were sent to Ken for his signature.

Despite finally taking action to end their marriage, Renee was unable to resist the hope that Ken would change his behavior, so she allowed him to spend the next few months moving back and forth between his home and a temporary residence. According to Renee, there were good times and bad times during this period. And, periodically, she would ask Ken why he hadn't signed the divorce papers. Chief among his excuses was the statement: "I've misplaced them."

At 4:00 a.m., after an evening in which Ken hadn't come home, Renee received a phone call from a police captain. He told her that her husband had been in an accident and that two officers were waiting at her front door to drive her to the hospital. The night before was "payday Wednesday"—an evening when a group of officers, including Ken, often traded some of their earnings for drinks at a bar on the department's training academy campus. (The practice has since been disbanded.)

"When I was escorted to the ER, I saw officers lined up behind the captain and they were all standing at attention. Tears were streaming down their faces," Renee said. "And then I was taken to see Ken's body." Renee knew that she was married to a man who had a job that could be dangerous—he carried a gun and worked in a crime-ridden neighborhood. But Ken wasn't killed on the job. Renee was told that he died as the result of an accident that occurred after he had consumed too much alcohol and then drove off on his motorcycle. Minutes later, his bike went off the road and Ken suffered a fatal head injury. In the pocket of his motorcycle

jacket, police found the divorce papers. They were unsigned.

"I've given a lot of thought to who I want to be now and in the future," Renee said. "I'm educating myself. I'm learning. I'm resourceful and I've realized that I'm strong. I'm committed to personal and professional growth. And I'm beginning to find my way. I will never stand in one place. Never."

# Sue
## Holloway

"Everyone said to me:
'Now you can do
whatever you want to do.'
But I no longer knew
what that was."

# Sue Holloway

Sue Holloway and Carl Hopkins had reached a lovely time in their lives. They had been married for 23 years and Sue, a successful 53-year-old businesswoman, had recently retired so that she and Carl could travel together and spend time on their favorite leisure pursuits. (Carl was 16 years older than Sue and had already made the switch from working as an engineer to toiling in his garden.) Sue wanted to dedicate some of her free time to climbing and trekking, two activities that interested and challenged her. But then things changed: Carl was diagnosed with Alzheimer's disease and all their plans were shelved.

Instead of climbing mountains or traveling to Borneo, Sue focused on becoming her husband's caregiver. She developed a routine that centered on Carl—encircling and protecting him as he gradually lost his memories and his functioning slowly declined. And then Carl developed pneumonia. In a matter of hours, he went from being a man who could walk on his own to one who couldn't; he went from being someone who could make his own breakfast and dress himself, to someone who didn't know where he was. As a result of his illness, Carl had to be hospitalized—and during his two-week stay, he was delusional and unable to brush his teeth or feed himself. Sue could no longer care for him at home and the hospital was unwilling to keep him any longer. Sue, who felt she was out of options, reluctantly transferred her husband to a small facility for people with Alzheimer's.

Once over the shock of his precipitous decline, Sue adapted. "I visited him daily and came prepared with activities we could do together," she said. "Church on Sundays, dinner out once a week, reading, talking, looking at photographs, a daily cup of coffee at Starbucks." Shortly after Carl had settled into his new living quarters, Sue requested permission to take him to a nearby hotel for an evening of dinner out and snuggling in. "It meant so much to me to sleep in bed with my husband...one more time," she said.

And then, one day Sue made her customary visit to the facility and saw her husband sitting on a sofa—smiling broadly—and holding hands with another resident, a woman named Vivian. "This is my girlfriend," he said.

Sue was immediately overcome with intense feelings of jealousy and could only cry in response to Carl and Vivian's obvious joy. "I thought I could handle it, but I couldn't," she said. And she wasn't proud of her response. After a little time and thought though, Sue's feelings evolved. "My initial turmoil dissipated when I observed how happy they were. It made me realize that even though this horrible disease had destroyed so much of their brains, their need for closeness and companionship remained." And just like that, Vivian's presence became part of their ever-changing lives.

Five days before his death, Sue was able to bring Carl back to the house they had shared for decades. Despite his severe dementia, when Sue said to him "You're home," he softly mouthed to her "I know."

After Carl died, Sue was at a loss for things to do. "I never really got back into a routine after his death," she said. "I had a lot of things scheduled each day, but it all seemed forced. Everyone said to me: 'Now you can do whatever you want to.' But I no longer knew what that was." For years, Sue had been laser-focused on Carl and his illness; he was virtually all she thought about, talked about and planned her days around. Now she struggled to redefine herself.

After reflecting on her growth during her days as a caregiver and celebrating her increased empathy, patience, and maturity, Sue decided to move forward by literally moving on. A year after Carl's passing, she sold their home and drove 2500 miles to a house she purchased in a small town she barely knew. "I was comfortable making such a big leap because I didn't think it was the last choice I would have in my lifetime. If things didn't work out, I could do something else," Sue said. But things did work out. "I stepped out of my comfort zone, hoping to find myself again. And I did," she said.

# Linda
## Halley

"When I enjoy myself,
I usually look up and say,
'Okay, Robin.' And then
I talk to him about it."

# Linda
## Halley

Linda and Robin Halley had been married for 21 years when cancer struck with a one-two punch. Robin was diagnosed first, with Stage IV lung cancer. Linda was diagnosed a month later, with breast cancer. The two, who were both 61 at the time, took turns caring for each other as they withstood repeated—and often debilitating—cancer treatments.

Robin underwent eight surgeries in five years and had countless rounds of chemotherapy. During the same period, Linda had three surgeries for her breast cancer, four months of chemo, two hip replacements and also surgery for a broken knee. "Fortunately, during this period we were never at our worst at the same time," Linda said.

The couple had many friends: people Robin and Linda knew since school, business associates, members of their clog dancing group, and neighbors who came to know each other through the Halley's "Annual Not-on-the-Fourth-of-July" summer party. But their primary cancer support group was small, consisting of just Linda's sister and one close friend. Linda kept their larger circle of friends connected to information about their health and activities through regular online updates.

Robin had every test, procedure and treatment that was available. But none of that, even with the limitations and discomfort caused by the illness, kept the pair from continuing to work and travel. And, despite the fact that only three percent of the people with his diagnosis survive the disease, the couple believed he would be among the tiny group that did. "We were really hopeful," Linda recalled, "and we refused to allow negativity to creep into our world. We didn't think our life together was going to end." But five years after his cancer was discovered, Robin died. In his home, surrounded by family and friends, Robin spoke his final words: "I'm done."

"I watched his soul leave," Linda said. "You could almost see it lift. I don't believe in God, and neither did Robin, but I do believe in the energy of the universe and I hope my energy mingles with his somewhere."

Linda Halley credits her two dogs, Bisoux and Chandler, with saving her life during the protracted grieving she experienced after her husband died. "I thought about my husband all the time. I still do. The only reason I survived was because of them," Linda said as she gazed maternally at the two Cavalier Spaniels who were sleeping soundly on a nearby bed. "I didn't function very well the first year after Robin's death," Linda said. "And if I didn't have the dogs, I probably wouldn't be here; we didn't have children… there wouldn't have been any reason to…"

Linda, who was a flight attendant at a time when such a job was considered glamorous and when flight attendants were called "stewardesses," describes herself as a people-person. But, in the throes of grief, she turned inward and excluded all but one human friend. "When Robin first died, I was filled with deep despair and excruciating pain interspersed with moments of numbness," Linda said. "I felt that every time I interacted normally with someone, I was only acting—while on the inside I was shrieking and screaming."

Only recently has Linda's depression started, gradually, to ease. Feeling secure and comfortable with her pets at her side, she began engaging in life outside her home. The first trips, with the dogs on a leash or in a stroller (the aging animals suffer from arthritis) were walks to a neighborhood café for coffee. The tail-wagging duo attracted company and made it easier for Linda to mingle and carry on light conversation. Soon, she felt up to taking additional steps. She spruced up her garden, made a few changes in her home, and began accepting invitations to attend movies or go to dinner with friends. "I'm starting to say, 'Yes' to things," she said. "When I enjoy myself, I usually look up and say, 'Okay, Robin.' And then I talk to him about it."

# Michele
## Linn

"He cried like a baby.
He was scared."

# Michele
## Linn

Before heading to Iraq, Staff Sgt. Aaron White and his wife, Michele Linn, sat together on their living room couch and watched the Academy Award-winning film *Black Hawk Down.* Aaron, who was 27 years old and assigned to a Marine helicopter squadron, put his head in his wife's lap and broke down in tears as he watched the gripping war scenes and helicopter crashes. "He cried like a baby," Michele said. "He was scared." It was the only time the Marine—who had joined the military after graduating high school and had wanted to fly since he was a child—expressed any concerns to Michele about his upcoming mission.

Aaron left for Iraq in March of 2003. Two months later, he and three other Marines from Camp Pendleton were flying in a CH-46 Sea Knight helicopter when it crashed into the Shatt al Hillah Canal south of Bagdad. All of the men on board died along with a fifth Marine who drowned after diving into the canal in an attempt to rescue them.

At the time of Aaron's death, Michele was with her parents in Texas celebrating their daughter Brianna's first birthday. Michele was watching CNN when breaking news about a fatal helicopter crash in Iraq appeared on a crawl at the bottom of the screen. Although she knew that the details on the ticker dovetailed with Aaron's equipment and location, she couldn't accept the possibility that he might have been involved in the fatal crash. Hours later, and free from worry, she was able to go to sleep. The Marines, after sending a team to Michele's Camp Pendleton home and finding no one home, sent a second team to Oklahoma to break the news of the crash to Aaron's parents. Michele was awakened a few hours later by her father (who had been called by Aaron's father) and told that her husband had been classified as "missing in action." The next day, after the bodies of the missing servicemen were retrieved from the canal, uniformed Marine officers and a chaplain were dispatched to the home of Michele's parents. That's when Michele was officially informed that Aaron was dead. She, at 27, was a widow.

Despite initial concerns about how she'd raise her daughter without a job or a college degree, and filled

with fears that she would end up homeless, Michele was allowed to continue living on the Camp Pendleton base for the next two years (rent-free for the first six months) and she used the educational benefits afforded military widows to earn a bachelor's degree in Criminal Justice (she went on to earn her MS through an online program). Although she receives numerous benefits for herself and Brianna, Michele had become frustrated by aspects of the military system and procedures (although, as the daughter of an Air Force Major, she was familiar with both). "I started having trouble after my CCAO [Casualty Calls Assistance Officer] was deployed to Iraq," Michele said. "My paperwork was getting lost and I wasn't

hearing back from people or getting my questions answered. I didn't receive Aaron's personal property or autopsy for years after I had requested them. So I started searching for answers myself." On the Internet, Michele came across the site for Gold Star Wives, a nonprofit organization that provides support to widows and widowers of military personnel and advocates to improve the benefits and services they receive.

"GSW had a chat room and I began bonding over computer screens and keyboards with a dozen or so local military widows," Michele recalled. "When we finally met in person there was a lot of crying and laughing. And I no longer felt alone." A few of the women decided to formalize the group so that they could reach out to other military widows who might be feeling isolated or struggling to understand the system. And that's how SSSG [Surviving Spouse Support Group] was born.

"I became involved because I had done tons of research, had resources, and knew where to turn for help," Michele said. And when the group appeared to be running out of leaders, and steam, she stepped in to make sure that it continued—and expanded. "I feel a sense of responsibility," she said, "I know what it's like to search for answers and support and I know I can help others who are in the same position I was in." Michele has a tattoo on the ankle of her right foot which she has systematically, and symbolically, been adding to over the years. A cherry blossom represents the time she and Aaron spent stationed in Japan, and a butterfly was added three years after his death. But perhaps the most significant addition to her tattoo is the quote that she chose to have placed on her ankle six years after the helicopter crash that ended her husband's life: "Freedom is not Free."

# Marilyn

## Colby

"The hospice facility
wasn't a place of sadness;
it was magical."

# Marilyn
## Colby

Ten days after Marty Colby's death, just as the sun was starting to set, his eldest stepson pulled a kayak across the sand and into the sea. A box containing Marty's remains rested on the floor of the kayak and following behind the boat, on surfboards, were another son and two grandchildren. Marty's widow, Marilyn, and other family members watched from the beach as birds screamed their early evening calls and seals and porpoises played in the ocean near the shore. As the brilliant yellow sun vanished from the pink sky, the biodegradable container containing Marty's ashes was placed in the water and slowly sank below the surface.

"It was an exceptionally beautiful evening," Marty's wife of 37 years, recalled. Marilyn had been widowed for one month and three weeks when she sat in her art-filled home overlooking the ocean discussing the evening her husband's ashes were lowered into the sea. "I wanted to watch the ceremony from the beach; I didn't want to go out in the kayak," she said. Marilyn was quiet for a few minutes and then added, "I wasn't there when Marty died, either."

Seventeen years Marilyn's senior, Marty had been in declining health for about a year before his death. While celebrating his 88th birthday, he suffered a fall from which he never recovered. "I didn't think he was going to die," Marilyn said while reaching for a tissue to dry her tears, "he had survived so much." After ten difficult days in the hospital, when it was clear that Marty wasn't going to pull through, he was moved to a hospice facility.

The tightness in Marilyn's face changed to a soft smile when the conversation shifted from talk of her husband's hospital stay to their hospice experience—she was by his side during both. "The hospice facility wasn't a place of sadness; it was magical," Marilyn said. "The nurses, doctors, psychologists, bereavement counselors, and musicians made us feel comfortable and comforted. They filled Marty's room with their smiles, their empathy, and their love. They were angels."

At about 10:00 p.m., on what would turn out to be the night Marty died, an exhausted Marilyn left the hospice facility. She arrived home to a ringing phone with a nurse on the line. Marilyn was advised that the end was near and that she should return immediately if she wanted to be with her husband when he passed. "I decided I didn't need to be there," Marilyn said emphatically, adding, "He had chosen this time for himself."

Marilyn had often heard that "people die when they choose to die." She was also told that it is not unusual for a spouse to stay by the side of their loved one only to find that he or she died after they left the room for a quick snack or a bathroom break. These were the stories that flashed through Marilyn's mind when she made her decision not to return.

"I didn't go back to the hospice facility. And I'm glad I didn't...I think his soul went to heaven before his body did," she said softly. And even though she chose not be on the boat with her husband's ashes, or at his side when he took his last breath, she has created her own ways of memorializing, remembering, and celebrating Marty.

"His favorite ties hang next to my shirts in my closet, and they always will," she said. And she now wears his wedding ring below her identical, but smaller, simple gold band. Every evening, as part of what has become a loving ritual, Marilyn moves Marty's ring to her middle finger so it won't fall off during a restless night of sleep. And then she climbs under the covers—on what used to be Marty's side of the bed.

# Coryl
## Crane

"Allan's part
of the fabric of my life
and just because he died
doesn't mean
that he's gone."

# Coryl Crane

"I was with him when he died," Coryl Crane said. "I was sitting with him and then suddenly he took his last breath and it seemed as if all the energy and spirit in his body just floated out of him. It was palpable. I couldn't see it, but I could feel it. I'd never seen him more relaxed or more beautiful. I reached out to touch him, but I didn't feel a need to hold him or hold on to him. He was no longer in his body. It was one of the most beautiful moments of my life. It reminded me of giving birth; life going in, life going out."

We spoke on a sunny morning in mid-May and Coryl, who is a master teacher in the Japanese martial art of Aikido, stood barefoot in her kitchen. She looked like a dancer as she moved with grace and a straight back around the room brewing tea and talking about the death of her husband, the internationally celebrated artist Allan Kaprow, whose overall physical and mental health had been deteriorating for several years before he died from cardiopulmonary failure and Parkinson's Disease. During their 28 years together, and 19 years as a married couple, Coryl and Allan focused their lives and their work on personal and artistic growth and self-awareness. But their relationship didn't always garner the same amount of attention that other aspects of their lives did; the pair often struggled to achieve the level of open and uncomplicated communication they both sought.

"During much of our marriage, we were dealing with things that sometimes got in the way of intimate conversation," Coryl said, referring—in part—to the challenges that often accompanied two demanding careers and the raising of a child (their son, Bram, was born when Coryl was 44 years old.) In addition, they were 16 years apart and from two different countries and backgrounds—they brought divergent communication styles and experiences to their partnership.

"Allan was brilliant and he occasionally used that brilliance to establish a distance between us. I thought there was some sort of holding back and it played into my insecurities. But towards the end of his life, he became vulnerable and was better able to express his love for me. And that freed me to experience and communicate the depth of my love for him. There was a deep, deep loss after he died. It was like an empty space that I had to live with and grow used to," she said.

After Allan's death, his widow—who is the trustee of his art and legacy—spent a lot of time with his work, much of which had been created before they met. And while representing Allan during a series of traveling exhibitions she also had lengthy discussions with many of his colleagues and former students. "Everyone remembered Allan when he was alive and dynamic and they wanted to talk to me about him," Coryl said. At that point, Allan—as an artist and teacher—became more alive to her and she was better able to step back and see his life in its entirety. "As my understanding of his art grew, so did my appreciation and love for him," she said. "My relationship with Allan has grown since his death and I can have the kinds of conversations with him now that I couldn't when he was alive. Allan's part of the fabric of my life and just because he died doesn't mean that he's gone."

After several months spent working on behalf of Allan's art (something she still does on occasion) Coryl's commitment to her dojo—the studio where she has taught Aikido for two decades—became even more passionate and purposeful (during her absence, her students ran the dojo until she was able to return). "I understand viscerally the finality of life, and there's a sense of urgency behind what I do now. I'm centered and mentally stronger than ever and I want to stay on this peak as long as I'm able to do so," said the 68-year-old with the 6th degree black belt. "There's no reason to crawl into a cave once we pass 60."

# Jennifer

## Congernaum

“Initially, I would say
things like,
‘Yeah, Jon died,
but it’s not a big deal.
I’m fine.’”

# Jennifer Congernaum

Jennifer Conger, a native of Southern California, was just 20 years old when, in 1980, she married Jon Naum, a 22-year-old emigrant from communist-led Romania. She was, she said, "enthralled by him" and had never met someone who was as exotic as he was. In addition to his foreign accent, good looks, intelligence, and creativity, Jennifer added that Jon also had a car, job, house, and maturity. By her own admission, though, Jennifer knew nothing about marriage; her expertise, she recalled, was in flirting, dating, and underage drinking. Still, seven months after they met, she married Jon in San Francisco. A year later, Jon would take his own life.

At first, the couple's marriage was easy and fun, and Jon's competence and gentle manner made Jennifer feel protected. Less than 12 months later, though, Jon lost a job he enjoyed and was unable to find satisfaction in his new position. And Jennifer was becoming bored and depressed. "Looking back," she said, "I should have recognized what Jon was going through, but at the time all I knew was that being married wasn't fun anymore." Jennifer wasn't equipped, she admitted, to deal with the changes and challenges in her marriage. Jennifer left San Francisco and returned to San Diego—to the sunshine and to the ease of being a single woman of 21. "During the last phone call Jon and I had, almost three weeks after I moved out, I told him that I didn't want to be married anymore and didn't want to live in a city without light. He asked me if I was sure, and then added 'Nobody is going to love you the way I do.'"

Despite their separation, the couple spoke to each other on the phone at least once a day. So when Jennifer was unable to reach Jon for two days, she became concerned and contacted one of his coworkers who—with the police—went to Jon's apartment. An officer called Jennifer from the scene to tell her that her husband had been found with his wrists slashed. He had taken his life immediately following his last phone conversation with Jennifer. And while Jon didn't leave a note, he did leave one final message. The initials "J+J" were found written in blood on a wall near where his body lay.

After Jon's death, Jennifer was filled with guilt and was wrestling with questions that were unanswered—and unasked. She felt that she had no one to discuss her intense emotions with. Her parents, she said, tried to be helpful but they wanted her to put the entire experience behind her, so she didn't think she could turn to them for guidance. "I went to live with Jon's parents in Connecticut for a few weeks, but I thought they were blaming me for their son's death so I went back home again. I was a kid; of course I thought my husband's suicide was my fault."

In the years that followed, Jennifer was involved in two serious relationships and had a son with each man. "Babies didn't scare me, marriage scared me," Jennifer said. "I start to panic if I think about the possibility of another husband dying before I do." At the age of 31, Jennifer began seeing a therapist after experiencing severe panic attacks (which, she subsequently learned, ran in her family). There was finally someone she felt free to talk with about the death of her young husband.

Slowly, Jennifer began exploring feelings she had buried for a decade. "Initially, I would say things like, 'Yeah, Jon died, but it's not a big deal. I'm fine,'" Jennifer said. With time and continued therapy, however, she realized that she wasn't to blame for Jon's suicide and that it was okay not only to miss him, but also to learn how to integrate the tragedy and sadness of his death into her life. "I don't think I could have come to those realizations, or had those kinds of conversations with a therapist, when was I was 21," she said.

From time to time, Jennifer still meets with her therapist. As does her second husband, Ernie Bornheimer, who is the father of her third son and the man she's been married to for 12 years. "My relationship with Ernie is built on trust and friendship and has only gotten better with time," Jennifer said. "And when we hit a rough spot, we talk about it and work together to find a solution."

Although a happily married mother of three, Jennifer still has a trunk stored under her house that's packed with her late husband's clothing, flyers from shows they saw together, and letters he wrote to her. She's moved that trunk from one residence to another...ten times. And, if she and Ernie move from their current home, the trunk will move with them.

# Barb
## Kurtz

"The choices were
to curl up and cry…
or get it done."

# Barb
## Kurtz

John Kurtz and his wife Barb had been married for 40 years when he stopped recognizing her. Three years after being diagnosed with Alzheimer's disease, at the age of 57, John mistook his wife for a stranger who had invaded his home and violated his space. Pre-Alzheimer's, John was a gentle and trusting man; post-Alzheimer's, he was paranoid, full of anger, fear, and potential violence.

Barbara Kurtz gazed out a window of her cozy mountain home at the vast and gorgeous valley below. She had been reminiscing about the man she met and fell in love with in seventh grade algebra class. A tear slipped down her face as she said, "I have a great life, but I'll miss my husband until the day I die." Prior to John's illness, the childless couple shared an active and relatively uncomplicated life. Barb was a veterinary technician at a wild animal park and her husband a self-employed machinist. She loved to ride her horse in the hills and he loved to putter in their barn and house. A line of framed photographs that hang in the couple's living room illustrate the life they once lived. In each image—whether it's just the two of them, or whether they're in the company of friends, or surrounded by animals—they're always laughing.

But there was no laughter the night that Barb realized that she could no longer manage a man who couldn't recognize the difference between his wife and an intruder. Fearing a physical assault, and not wanting their situation to escalate to the point of possible police intervention, Barb called John's doctor for help. Her husband was moved to a psychiatric behavioral unit for evaluation and an analysis of his medications; from there he was transferred to an Alzheimer's facility. Even though she understood the reality of their situation, Barb was nevertheless filled with guilt and convinced she was abandoning the man she had vowed to stand by—in sickness and in health.

Four months before his death, Barb brought John home. In his last stage of Alzheimer's, he was no longer a danger to himself or his wife. There he remained in a hospital bed, unmoving and unseeing,

next to the window with the spectacular view. His junior high sweetheart was by his side. "I felt some relief when he died," Barb confessed, "he was no longer limited by the disease or confined to bed, and I was never going to abandon him again."

Barb, who likes her own company (along with that of her three dogs, five goats, and a parrot), is very proud of her newly revealed self-sufficiency and strength. While she was always organized and efficient, John was the person who took care of things around their house. "Why should I climb a ladder when he could?" she asked. And then she learned just how much she could do. When a raging wildfire threatened to destroy her home, Barb methodically gathered together all her animals, put them in her car, and calmly evacuated as television news copters circled overhead. When it was safe to return and rebuild, she (along with her beloved animals) lived for five months in a trailer on her property while a new house was assembled. "I knew John would have been proud of the way I worked with the inspectors and contractors," Barb said, "but, really, the choices were to curl up and cry...or get it done."

While reflecting on the ways she has grown, the newly independent widow said that she had been touched by the film *Mrs. Palfrey at the Claremont*. In her journal, Barb captured the moment in which the main character spoke about moving on after the death of a spouse:

> What he did by dying before me was to make me call on strengths I never knew I had, to appreciate independence, and not to fear the approach of my own last days on earth. Most of my life I have been somebody's daughter and somebody's wife. I would like to spend the rest of my life being simply myself.

"That just about sums it up for me," said Barb.

# Different Types of Losses Lead to Different Types of Bereavement Challenges

Michele Reiss, PhD

Loss and grief are small, simple sounding words and yet they represent complex and powerful life experiences. Grief is a universal phenomenon. It is a normal and mostly inevitable part of life and loving. After all, the only way to avoid grief is to never open up your heart to another. But for most of us, life will encompass both hellos and good-byes...

Grief is not only universal, it is also comprised of a series of somewhat predictable stages or phases that each of us will go through in some fashion as we cope with the loss of a loved one. And yet, grief is also a highly personal and individualized journey. There is not one right way to grieve and each of us will do so differently. In fact, if you experience more than one important loss in your life, each of those bereavement experiences may be different as well.

The variables that determine your individualized grief experience are many but usually include: one's basic personality inclinations, a person's cultural background and spiritual beliefs, the specific circumstances of the loss, the nature of the relationship to the lost loved one, prior experiences with illness or loss, other concurrent stresses that might unfortunately exist, and the degree to which we have support while we grieve. Because of these overlapping factors, reactions to loss are different not only among strangers but even among family members who are grieving the loss of a shared family member. These bereaved family members have lost the same special person, but each individual will make the journey through bereavement in their own particular way.

The specific circumstance of a loss is a factor worthy of further attention. There is no easy way to lose a loved one, but there are different loss experiences that lead to different bereavement challenges. For example, some losses are expected following a long, and possibly drawn out, chronic illness. Other losses are totally unexpected—often the end result of either a very acute medical event such as a massive heart attack, or stroke, or a lethal accident. Of course, you may also experience a bit of both if your loved one is chronically ill but unexpectedly takes a proverbial "turn for the worse."

Experiencing an expected loss theoretically gives one time to prepare and even to say good-bye. But witnessing a loved one struggle through a debilitating chronic illness is a truly heartrending experience. Being your partner's caretaker during a chronic illness is certainly a privilege and a statement of great love, but it is also physically exhausting and emotionally depleting. Somehow one has to find the time and energy and strength to support an ailing loved one, yet also cope with one's own sadness and fear at the prospect of being left. In many ways, this type of loss, over time, is like saying a series of good-byes over and over again as one gets closer to the final leave-taking. And yet, grief theorists and therapists would remind us that having this time to say good-bye, to hopefully leave nothing unsaid, is a precious opportunity despite the inherent hardships of bearing witness to a loved one's decline. This so-called "anticipatory grieving" does not necessarily lighten the grief that is yet to come, but it does give you warning and perhaps time to prepare and begin getting ready for whatever lies ahead.

Those who experience sudden, unanticipated losses have no warning—no time to prepare, and perhaps most importantly, no opportunity to say that last I love you, much less good-bye. Sudden losses come in many forms. In addition to the acute medical conditions and accidents mentioned above, violent crime, suicide, and natural disasters such as fires, floods, etc. all leave horribly unanticipated losses in their wake.

Bearing witness to a spouse's suffering over the course of a chronic illness may understandably lead to a sense of helplessness. Losing a husband or wife to a seemingly senseless event simply because they were in the wrong place at the wrong time may, at least temporarily, shake to the core our illusions of a safe and predictable world. Losing a partner or significant other unexpectedly also means that immediate and difficult decisions related to autopsies and funerals are often made while in a state of dazed shock, leaving room to second-guess those decisions later. In these unanticipated circumstances, there also hasn't been an opportunity to even begin to contemplate the potential personal, financial, and lifestyle changes that might now lie ahead.

Most of us experience an initial period of disbelief when we lose a loved one. This is true whether that illness is expected or not. Somehow, even with warning, the notion that our life partner is now truly gone, is just really hard to process. ("I just can't believe it. I keep waiting to wake up and find out this was just a bad dream.") Those that are dealing with unexpected losses, may understandably encounter a more prolonged period of disbelief. Both those having experienced a sudden loss and those coping with the loss of a loved one after a prolonged illness, will have to find a way, over time, to make peace with their loved one's suffering. And their own.

There is truly no easy, suffering-free way to lose a spouse. But different types of losses do lead to different bereavement experiences and challenges. However, all those who are grieving a loss will need to find some way to say to themselves, "This is not the life that I planned for or even desired, but it is still my life and worth living. I need to find a way through this: and over time I will." Coping with grief takes time. I wish there were shortcuts but I don't think there are. Amazingly, time does heal, but it usually takes much more time than any of us would have imagined or desired. So to begin with, anyone grieving needs to be patient with themselves, whether others around them are similarly patient or not.

Regardless of the circumstances of any particular grief, sometimes finding others who are coping with (and surviving) similar challenges is both useful and encouraging. We all need and deserve credible support during the hard times. It is important, however, to let those around you who care and want to help, know what kinds of help you might find most useful. Otherwise you might find yourself the recipient of a good deal of well-intended but not particularly useful advice. Ultimately you will have to use your own judgment about what is, or is not, helpful to you, but finding folks who care and understand is an important step in the process of moving through your grief. Ultimately, whether this support comes from family, friends, fellow widows/widowers, a therapist or a support group, or an illuminating book such as *One Foot Forward* doesn't matter. It is important to find support and use it until things get easier. And they will.

Last, but certainly not least, consciously reminding yourself to remain aware of what you still have can be a powerful flashlight through the darkness. This is not a denial of what has been lost; it is simply a choice to also acknowledge that everything you still have matters. Initially it will seem to not make much difference, but eventually it will provide needed comfort. Each bereavement is unique, but so are each of you and the gift of you is worth all of this effort.

# Acknowledgments

This book would not have happened without the generosity of the people who shared—bravely and honestly—their experiences as widows and widowers. I thank them for granting me their trust and for allowing us to benefit from their stories and to learn from their experiences. I'm honored to have spent time with each of them.

*One Foot Forward* is in your hands now because many people believed in the project and supported it by introducing me to friends who were widowed, by reading early drafts, by connecting me to professionals in the field of bereavement and end-of-life issues, by sharing their personal experiences with grief, and by being there to listen to my ideas and offer their own in return.

The following people graciously contributed to this project in a variety of significant ways—a big hug and warm thanks go to: Louise Beckerman, Susan Bird, Brian Braff, Joyce Camiel, John Campbell, Noreen Carrington, Katie Collins, Mariacecilia Comunale, Richard Della Penna, Charles A. Corr, Jeffrey Epstein, Janet Evans, Paul Fredricks, Bonnie Hall, Judy Issokson, Naomi Kelman, Devra Korwin, Donna La Bonte, Frank Martin, Joe McNally, Michael D. Pierschbacher, Chris Sicola, Jayne Slade, Olga Stephens, Alix Taylor, Lorie Van Tilburg, Roberto Velasquez, and Kathleen Webber. A special shout-out goes to Brittany Comunale who was my intern until Brown University claimed her time and attention. Brittany is talented, responsible, and an absolute joy to work with.

Once again, I get to thank the team at powerHouse Books. I was fortunate to work with them on *I Still Do* and I am delighted to work with them again on *One Foot Forward*. Special recognition goes to: Craig Cohen, Wes Del Val, Will Luckman, Krzysztof Poluchowicz, Nina Ventura, and—of course—Daniel Power.

Personally and professionally, I'm extremely grateful to my talented daughter, Jennifer Fox Armour, who has encouraged, supported, and worked with me throughout the creation of *One Foot Forward*. Jennifer is an observant writer and photographer and has served as my sounding board and editor. Working with her has been a privilege, a gift, and a blast. And *One Foot Forward* is a better book because of her considerable abilities. I love you, Jennifer.

And to my family: Jennifer Fox Armour, Brian Fox, Hanna Armour, Ian Armour, Rik Armour, and Lindsay Sterling—my world is brighter, richer, and more fun because you're in it.